THE SMART KID'S GUIDE TO

Knowing
What to Say

BY M. J. COSSON • ILLUSTRATED BY RONNIE ROONEY

The Child's World

Published by The Child's World®
1980 Lookout Drive • Mankato, MN 56003-1705
800-599-READ • www.childsworld.com

Acknowledgments
The Child's World®: Mary Berendes, Publishing Director
Content Adviser: Philip C. Rodkin, Professor of Child
Development, Departments of Educational Psychology and
Psychology, University of Illinois
The Design Lab: Design
Red Line Editorial: Editorial Direction
Amnet: Production

Photographs © Shutterstock Images, cover, 1, 4; Thinkstock, 8,
14, 16, 22; iStock/Thinkstock, 10, 20, 23, 27, 28

ISBN 9781626873438
LCCN 2014930682

Printed in the United States of America
Mankato, MN
July, 2014
PA02224

ABOUT THE AUTHOR

M. J. Cosson was born in Des Moines, Iowa. She has worked as a teacher, editor, writer, and artist. She lives in Texas with her husband and pets.

ABOUT THE ILLUSTRATOR

Ronnie Rooney took art classes constantly as a child. She was always drawing and painting at her mom's kitchen table. She got her BFA in painting from the University of Massachusetts at Amherst and her MFA in illustration from the Savannah College of Art and Design in Savannah, Georgia. Ronnie lives on a U.S. Army base with her infantryman husband and two small children. Ronnie hopes to pass on her love of art and sports to her kids.

CONTENTS

How We Talk

*You will get better at talking to people
if you practice.*

There is a saying: "Has the cat got your tongue?"
It means, "Have you nothing to say?" Sometimes it
is really hard to know what to say. Some situations
might leave us feeling like a cat has got our tongue.

Knowing what to say is important. How we speak to each other makes a difference. We can be **supportive**, kind, and helpful. Or we can be **disrespectful** and hurt or ignore others' feelings.

Conversation is an art we learn. Anyone can learn to be good at it. Listen carefully to what others say. Then think about what you will say. Finally, say it in the best way you can at that moment.

Later, you might think of a better way to say something. It's okay that you couldn't think of it at the time. Your **body language**, the expression on your face, and your tone of voice helped get your message across. Your **intentions** were probably understood.

The more you work at something, the better you get. This is true with conversation. Practice the conversations in this book. Then have a conversation with a friend or trusted adult. You will get better at knowing what to say if you practice.

CHAPTER 1

When You Want Something

What do you do if you want something or want to do something? Do you keep it to yourself and figure it out on your own? Or do you tell someone who might be able to help you? You probably do both. If you

are looking for help from someone else, you need to
ask directly. Sometimes you need to **compromise**.
What would you do in the following situations?

*Jayna and Gavin are sister and brother. They are playing
with tiny snap-together blocks. They both reach for the same
block at the same time.*

Gavin: I need that piece. It goes right here. See?
It's part of my car.

Jayna: I need it to finish this side of my castle.

Gavin: Can't you find another piece that works?

Jayna: Why can't you find another piece?

Gavin: I looked. That's the only one, and I have to
have it.

Jayna: Okay. I guess if I make my castle bigger, I
won't need that piece. You can have it.

Gavin: Thank you. I owe you one.

Jayna and Gavin talk through the problem.
They each explain their need. They look for a
solution together. Jayna compromises. Gavin lets her
know he appreciates what she did for him.

Have you met your neighbors? Ask your family to introduce you if you haven't.

Jack is saving money to buy a tablet computer. He needs to earn a few more dollars. Jack is walking past his neighbor's house. They wave at each other.

Mrs. Ngu: Hi, Jack.

Jack: Hi, Mrs. Ngu! How are you?

Mrs. Ngu: I'm fine. And you?

Jack: Good! I've noticed you have a lot of leaves in your yard. Would you like some help with raking? I wouldn't charge very much.

Mrs. Ngu: How much would you charge?

Jack: How about five dollars?

Mrs. Ngu: I can afford that. Thank you, Jack. And I have some cookies for when you are done.

Jack: Okay, Mrs. Ngu. Thanks. I'll go tell my mom and be right back. See you soon!

Jack smiles and waves back at Mrs. Ngu. Jack speaks clearly. He notices the leaves and asks about them. He sets a fair price for his work. Jack and Mrs. Ngu both say thank you. Instead of just walking away, Jack ends on a friendly note.

Kyla and her mom are shopping for school clothes. Kyla has found a top she likes, but it is expensive.

Kyla: Mom, can I have this purple top?

Mom: No, Kyla. It costs way too much. Here's a cute top. It's on sale.

Kyla: It's not the right purple to go with my jeans.

How do you ask for something you want?

Mom: Most purples look good together. Why don't you try it on? (Kyla tries on the top.)

Kyla: You're right. It looks good! May I have it?

Mom: Yes, I can afford that top.

Kyla: Thanks, Mom!

Kyla asks her mom for the expensive top. She does not whine or beg. She listens to what her mom says. She puts herself in her mom's place and thinks about price. She compromises. She asks her mom if she can have the less expensive top. She thanks her for it.

Here are some things you can do to get what you want and also respect others' wishes.

1. Listen to the other person. Do not interrupt. When there is a pause, it is your turn to talk.
2. Choose your words carefully. If you want something, state it clearly.
3. Be kind and show respect. Think about how the other person feels.
4. Compromise.
5. Say thank you.

CHAPTER 2

When Someone Is Sad or Hurting

If you have ever felt sad or scared, you know that it helps to have a caring friend. You can be that caring friend just by being there. You can also learn ways to talk to a friend who is hurting. Have you ever been in situations like these?

Anna's grandpa is going to have heart surgery tomorrow. Anna and her mom have stopped by the hospital to wish him well.

Anna: Hi, Grandpa!

Grandpa: Hi, sweetie. How is my favorite girl today?

Anna: I'm okay. And I know after tomorrow, you will be okay, too.

Grandpa: I like that positive thinking. Could you share it with me?

Anna: Sure! I can share it with a big hug. (She hugs her grandpa.)

Grandpa: That was nice. I feel better already!

Anna puts herself in her grandpa's place and shows she cares about him. She is positive. She feels good because she has made her grandpa feel better.

What else could Anna say to make her Grandpa feel better? She could try to take his mind off his troubles. She might say that she looks forward to going fishing with him soon. She could tell him something nice or funny that happened to her in school.

Ty and Toby are walking home from school. Toby usually talks a lot. But today he is very quiet.

Ty: You seem kind of sad today, Toby.

Toby: My mom and dad told us they're getting a divorce. Dad moved out yesterday.

What would you say to cheer up a friend?
Or help a friend through hard times?

Ty: Gosh, I'm sorry. That's got to be really hard.

Toby: It is. My mom is so sad. She isn't paying attention to us. And I don't know when I'll see Dad again.

Ty: I don't know what I'd do if my parents got a divorce. I know it's not the same, but you can come to my house. You, me, and my dad can play three-way catch. Or just watch a movie.

Toby: Thanks. It means a lot to me.

Ty does a good job of noticing Toby's mood. He does not ask embarrassing or nosy questions. He does let his friend know that he cares. Ty knows he can't fix the problem. So he offers his house and his dad to help Toby feel better.

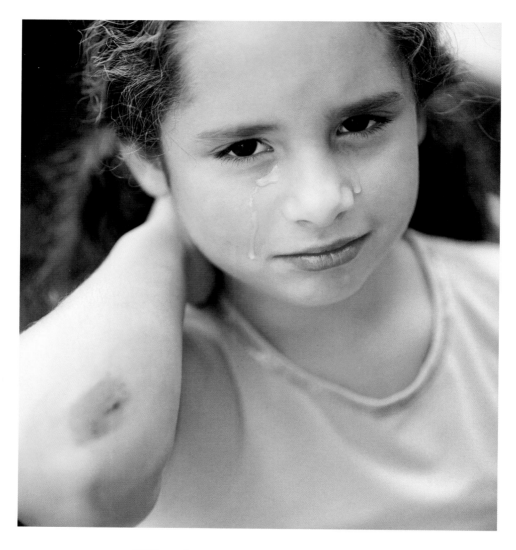

What do you say if a friend gets hurt?

*Bethany and Tristan are playing tag on the school
playground. Bethany is running. She trips over a tree root and
falls down hard. She has hurt her arm and is trying not to cry.*

Tristan: Are you okay, Bethany?

Bethany: Yes. Well, no. I hurt my arm.

Tristan: Oh, I see it is bleeding a little bit. Can you stand up and walk?

Bethany: Yes.

Tristan: I will help you get to the nurse.

Bethany: Thank you.

Tristan sees that Bethany is hurt. He does not say, "Tag, you're it." He does not laugh or run away. Instead he asks if she is okay. He is polite. He helps her to the nurse's office. Bethany says thank you to Tristan.

Here are some ways to show someone you care:
1. Talk in an even voice and tone.
2. Put yourself in the other person's place and think how he or she feels.
3. Use questions to help the other person talk. But do not ask nosy or embarrassing questions.
4. Listen carefully to what the other person says.
5. Say things that will not hurt the other person's feelings.
6. Use body language such as a hug or pat on the back to show you care.

CHAPTER 3
When Someone Has Been Kind

Being **courteous** is easy once you get used to doing it. Saying please and thank you is a start. What else do you say when someone does something nice for you?

Omri's aunt Julia just handed him a present. He is opening it now.

Omri: Oh, it's a shirt.

Aunt Julia: I just love that neon orange color. It will look good with your dark hair. Try it on!

Omri: Okay. (He pulls on the shirt over his T-shirt.)

Aunt Julia: Oh, yes, it looks great on you! It is for you to wear to the state fair. You will not get lost in the crowd!

Omri: Thank you, Aunt Julia. You take such good care of me!

Omri does not like the shirt. He says thanks to his aunt because it is polite. He wants her to feel good about her gift. He smiles. When he finds out that she got the shirt in the bright color for a purpose, he adds that to his words of thanks.

What can you say if someone hurts your feelings?
Or if you hurt someone else's feelings by accident?

*Averie and Leo are playing hide-and-seek. Averie
is well hidden. Leo says something that she isn't sure
is a compliment.*

Leo: Are you still around here? Can you give me a
clue? I've been looking for ten minutes.

Averie: Here I am! (She pops out from the pillows
on the couch.)

Leo: I looked there three times!

Averie: I just folded myself up and tried to look like a pillow.

Leo: You are wearing the same gray as the pillows. You are as small as a mouse! And you kind of look like one, too.

Averie: There are lots of good things about being small. And mice are cute, so I will take that as a compliment. Thanks! Now it's your turn to hide.

Leo might be upset that he could not find Averie. He might say that she is small and looks like a mouse to make her feel bad. Or he might mean it as a compliment. Averie decides to be positive about it. She just says thanks and moves on with the game.

What did you say the last time someone complimented you?

Hendry's teacher has asked him to stay in the classroom while others go out for recess today.

Hendry: Am I in trouble?

Teacher: Hendry, I've noticed that you are not talking or acting up in class. I just wanted to thank you for the good behavior. The more you pay attention in class, the more you will learn. So, good work! You can go outside now.

Hendry: Oh! Well, thank you!

At first, Hendry assumes he knows why his teacher wants to talk. But he listens to his teacher. And his teacher surprises him. Hendry says the right thing—thanks! It helps to make eye contact and smile when you say it. Often, that is all that is needed.

Try being thankful every day. Be thankful for what you have. Do not take gifts, compliments, or nice gestures for granted. Enjoy the compliment, help, or gift. Saying please and thank you can help you to feel thankful.

CHAPTER 4

When Something Is Hard to Say

It is often hard to find the right words to say.
It is especially hard when you have to stand up to
someone. You might disagree with what the other
person says or does. The other person might even be
a bully. Choose your words carefully. Say what you

need to say in a kind and helpful way. How would you handle these situations?

Zack and Miles are walking home from school.
   Zack: You've got that new video game, right? I want to come over to your house to play it.
   Miles: My mom won't be home for half an hour. No other kids are allowed.
   Zack: So she'll never know.
   Miles: I have to check in with my next-door neighbor. She lets me in the house.
   Zack: I'll just hide around the corner until she is gone.
   Miles: No, Zack. Sorry. You can't come to my house right now. But I can ask my mom if you can come over later, after she is home.

   Miles tells Zack no. He is firm. He follows the rules of his house. He is also kind to Zack, though.

Sari and Layla are sitting in the school lunchroom.

Layla: Did you see what Cori wore today? It's too big for her. I saw her sister wear it last year.

Sari: My mom buys my clothes a little too big so I can wear them longer. See, my jeans are rolled up.

Layla: Yes, but at least you don't wear hand-me-downs.

Sari: Well, actually, I do. I get clothes from my cousin. She goes to another school, so you haven't seen them before.

Layla: You didn't need to tell me that.

Sari: Well, there's nothing wrong with it. I don't think you should judge Cori by her clothes. She is fun to talk to. I like her. What difference do clothes make?

Layla: Clothes matter to me. Besides, Cori hardly ever talks to anybody. She doesn't have any friends.

Sari: Maybe she is shy. We should try to talk to her. Then we can be her friends. She is eating all alone. Let's ask her to join us.

Layla: Okay. Maybe she will be fun to talk to.

*Have you ever had to disagree with your friends? Was
it hard for you to do it? What did you say?*

Sari does something very hard. She stands up to
her friend about two things. She lets Layla know how
she feels about clothes. And she gets Layla to agree
to eat lunch with Cori.

*You can tell others to stop if they are
making you uncomfortable.*

*Bella is waiting for the school bus. Trey sneaks up behind
her and says, "Boo!" Bella jumps.*

Bella: Yikes!

Trey: Ha! I scared you.

Bella: Well, please don't do it again.

Trey: Oh, don't be a big baby. Are you going to
cry about it?

Bella: No. I guess it was kind of funny. But only
for you, not for me.

Trey: Well, get over it. You know I can really scare you if I want to.

Bella: I'm glad the bus is here, because I don't want to be around you anymore.

Bella stands up to Trey and lets him know she does not like how he is acting. She then tries to make a small thing of what seems to her like bullying. When Trey makes a threat, Bella gets out of the situation. She can also tell an adult if Trey doesn't stop.

Practice saying the right thing. Make a list of hard topics to talk about. Think about what you would say for each topic on the list. Write down some words that you could use. Practice talking about these things with a friend or trusted adult. Make up conversations with yourself, too.

TOP TEN THINGS TO KNOW

1. Smile.
2. Speak clearly.
3. Look the other person in the eye.
4. Listen.
5. Choose your words carefully.
6. Think of the other person.
7. Be honest, but be kind.
8. Ask questions to help the other person talk.
9. If you disagree, say so in a kind way.
10. Do not put up with bullying. Tell an adult.

GLOSSARY

body language (BAH-dee LANG-gwij) Body language is the way you hold your body that shows others how you feel. Your body language can show if you are happy or sad.

compromise (KAM-pruh-mize) To compromise is to agree on something so that each side gets part of what it wants. Sometimes you have to compromise about something you want.

conversation (kahn-ver-SAY-shun) A conversation is talking with another person. Have a conversation to get to know someone.

courteous (KUR-tee-uhs) Being courteous is showing respect for and good manners to others. It is courteous to get the door when someone else's hands are full.

disrespectful (dis-ri-SPEKT-ful) Someone who is disrespectful is not showing respect or kindness. It is disrespectful to borrow someone else's things without getting permission first.

intentions (in-TEN-shuns) Your intentions are what you meant or what you mean to do. People will understand if you have good intentions.

supportive (suh-POR-tive) Someone who is supportive is helpful or comforting. A supportive person listens when a friend is upset.

BOOKS

Criswell, Patti Kelley. *A Smart Girl's Guide to Knowing What to Say: Finding the Words to Fit Any Situation*. Middleton, WI: American Girl Publishing, 2011.

Ludwig, Trudy. *Trouble Talk*. Berkeley, CA: Tricycle Press, 2008.

Verdick, Elizabeth. *Words Are Not for Hurting*. Minneapolis, MN: Free Spirit Publishing, 2009.

WEB SITES

Visit our Web site for links about knowing what to say:
childsworld.com/links
Note to Parents, Teachers, and Librarians:
We routinely verify our Web links to make sure they are safe and active sites. So encourage your readers to check them out!

INDEX

11/15